THE MONSTER IS REAL

THE MONSTER IS REAL

HOW TO FACE YOUR FEARS AND ELIMINATE THEM FOREVER

YEHUDA BERG

For further information:

The Kabbalah Centre
155 E. 48th St., New York, NY 10017
1062 S. Robertson Blvd., Los Angeles, CA 90035

1.800.Kabbalah www.kabbalah.com

First Edition
June 2005
Printed in USA
ISBN 1-57189-307-5

Design: Hyun Min Lee

DEDICATION

To all those who have suffered from debilitating fears all their lives: I hope that the wisdom in these pages gives you the tools and the power to finally free yourself from the prison that holds you captive. You are not alone.

TABLE OF CONTENTS

ACKNOWLEDGMENTS

I would like to thank the many people who have made this book possible.

First and foremost, Rav and Karen Berg, my parents and teachers. I will be forever thankful for your continual guidance, wisdom, and unconditional support. I am just one of the many whom you have touched with your love and wisdom.

Michael Berg, my brother, for your constant support and friendship, and for your vision and strength. Your presence in my life inspires me to become the best that I can be.

My wife, Michal, for your love and commitment; for your silent power; for your beauty, clarity, and uncomplicated ways. You are the strong foundation that gives me the security to soar.

David, Moshe, Channa, and Yakov, the precious gifts in my life who remind me every day how much there is to be done to ensure that tomorrow will be better than today.

Billy Phillips, one of my closest friends, for your help in making this book possible. The contribution you make to The Kabbalah Centre every day and in so many ways is appreciated far more than you could possibly know.

To Hyun Lee, Christian Witkin, and Esther Sibilia, whose contributions made the physical quality and integrity of everything we do live up to the spiritual heritage of this incredible wisdom that has been passed on to me by my father, Rav Berg.

I want to thank Rich Freese, Eric Kettunen, and all the team at PGW for their vision and support. Your proactive efficiency gives us the confidence to produce more and more books on Kabbalah so that the world can benefit from this amazing wisdom.

To all the Chevre at The Kabbalah Centres worldwide—the evenings we share together in study fuel my passion to bring the power of Kabbalah to the world. You are a part of me and my family no matter where you might be.

To the students who study Kabbalah all over the world—your desire to learn, to improve your lives, and to share with the world is an inspiration. The miracles I hear from you every day make everything I do worthwhile.

An old Cherokee was teaching his young grandson one of life's most important lessons. He told the young boy the following parable:

"There is a fight going on inside each of us. It is a terrible fight between two wolves," he said.

"One wolf is evil. He is anger, rage, envy, regret, greed, arrogance, self-pity, guilt, resentment, lies, false pride, superiority, and ego. The second wolf is good. He is joy, peace, love, hope, serenity, humility, kindness, empathy, truth, compassion, and faith."

The grandson thought about this for a moment. Then he asked his grandfather, "Which wolf will win this fight?"

The old Cherokee simply replied, "The one you feed."

Part One

THE ORIGINS OF FEAR

INTRODUCTION

If you're like most people, you probably think of anxiety and panic attacks as modern ailments stemming from the stress in your hectic life. Not true. Exaggerated fear has been part of the human experience since the dawn of existence. For instance, the word *panic* is derived from Pan, the name of an ancient Greek god who was said to cause intense and sudden mindless fear. The Greeks wrote about people who were afraid to leave their homes and enter public places; they called such people agoraphobics. Over 1,000 years ago, Vikings used deer urine to create chemical stimulants designed to banish fear. A militant Muslim sect in the 11th century was known as "Hashshashin" because they used hashish before battle to reduce fear. Queen Elizabeth I was known as the Red Rose of England, but, ironically, Her Majesty suffered from a fear of flowers known as anthophobia.

Fear has been around a long, long time. But guess what? So has an ancient technology that promises the

THE **MONSTER** IS REAL

power to cure your fears. Unfortunately, it has been locked away in ancient vaults for the last two millennia. Only recently did it come to light. The solution for eradicating fear is found in the ancient technology known as Kabbalah, the oldest wisdom in the world. The purpose of this book is to share Kabbalah's solution with everyone who suffers from any kind of fear-related ailment. If you're fortunate enough to be free of anxiety and panic, then this book is not for you. But if fear causes you any unnecessary discomfort or pain, be it minor or extreme, get ready to conquer this age-old problem once and for all.

FEAR COMES IN ASSORTED FLAVORS

Fear comes in many forms. The world of psychiatry has created a host of names to designate every fear-related ailment. Just take a look at this partial list: Dystychiphobia is a fear of accidents. Hemophobia refers to a fear of blood. Taphephobia is a fear of being buried alive. Illyngophobia is when you have a fear of vertigo and getting dizzy. You're called misophobic when you have a fear of contamination from dirt and germs. Aviophobia is a common one: it's a fear of flying. Some people are afraid of France; this fear is called Francophobia. Some people have a fear of flutes (yes, the musical instruments); it's called aulophobia. Some people are even afraid of very long words. The name for this is hippopotomonstrosesquippedaliophobia. (And whoever dreamed that one up had a cruel sense of humor!)

If, by chance, you're afraid about becoming afraid of all the above-mentioned fears, you could very well be afflicted with something called panophobia, which is defined as a persistent, abnormal, and irrational fear of everything.

In response to the fears and phobias that haunt you in your daily life, doctors often prescribe pills. Psychiatrists will put you on their couches. Psychologists will hypnotize you or prescribe treatments like cognitive behavioral therapy.

According to Kabbalah, drugs and psychotherapy might assist you in managing your anxieties, but they cannot cure them completely. Only when you get to the underlying root cause of your fears can you ever hope to eradicate the phobias that cripple your life. (This root cause is intimately intertwined with the meaning and purpose of your life, which we'll explore shortly.)

Psychotherapist Jamie Greene, a member of the Southern California Psychoanalytic Institute, has been treating anxiety disorders for 15 years. Five years ago he was introduced to the technology of Kabbalah and has been using it to treat patients ever since. As Greene puts it,

*The difference between the two approaches
is profound. Psychotherapy treats symptoms.
Kabbalah addresses the core issue.*

*The conventional approach is to get people
back to their best level of functioning before
their symptoms occurred. But even when you
succeed, you are still not treating the cause
of their fears. This leaves room for reoccur-
rence. Even the subconscious mind does not
probe to the level of the soul, or the true reality. One of my patients had panic attacks for
20 years. She was undergoing treatments to
cope with and reduce her symptoms. Then I
introduced her to Kabbalah. After three ses-
sions, she never had a panic attack again.
What I experienced with my other patients
was equally profound. I have given up traditional practice and now utilize Kabbalah full
time in treating anxiety disorders.*

One Cause

Despite all the complex names now used to officially label fears, the ancient wisdom of Kabbalah says there is only *one* true cause. Whatever form a fear may take, a single underlying seed is the basis for its existence.

Kabbalah refers to that underlying cause as *the monster*.

AFRAID OF THE MONSTER

As a child, you were probably afraid of monsters, but your parents assured you that there was no such thing.

Wrong. The monster is real.

You were probably told that there was nothing to be afraid of. On the contrary, you *should* be afraid. In fact, you should be very afraid. Before you panic, you should know that this monster is not the mythical creature you feared so deeply as a child. He is not lurking in your closet or preparing to leap out from under your bed. This monster is *in your bed*. In fact, *he's inside of you!* And he's been there since the day you were born. This monster was not implanted by some diabolical modern-day Frankenstein. He was actually conjured up by the master of the universe, the force you know as God or the Creator.

But why?

Why would a God that you know to be compassionate and all-loving place such a frightening creature inside of you? *Because you asked Him to.* Exactly *why* you asked to have such a terrifying entity implanted within you will be explained shortly.

THE MONSTER CALLED EGO

Another term for the monster I've been describing is "the ego." According to Kabbalah, ego is not just someone's inflated view of himself or herself. Yes, conceit, self-importance, and overconfidence are part of ego. But ego also includes low self-esteem, shyness, and feelings of inferiority.

The ego creates extroverts and introverts. Ego makes you feel like you are the best, and it makes you feel like you are the worst. It grows when you feed it, and then it converts its energy into feelings of conceit or feelings of inferiority.

Can you recall a time in your life when you knew something was extremely bad for you—*but you went ahead and did it anyway?* The voice that coaxed you into negative behavior is also ego.

Do you remember a time when you knew for certain that a particular activity would be beneficial and positive for your life—*but then you didn't do it?* You delayed it, you convinced yourself to put it off, and then you totally forgot about it? That voice of procrastination is defined as ego, too.

In a nutshell, the best way to understand ego, according to Kabbalah, is to recognize that 99% of your everyday behavior follows the dictates of ego.

The 24-Hour Broadcast

Imagine two radios side by side. One is broadcasting rock music, and the other is broadcasting classical. The radio broadcasting the rock music is blaring, the volume cranked up high. The radio broadcasting the classical music is barely audible. The best way to hear the classical music is to shut off the other radio.

Life works the same way. Like those two radios, your brain picks up signals from both your ego and your soul. The volume on EGO 99.9 is pumped up to the maximum and it plays monster hits 24 hours a day. SOUL FM radio is set at a low volume. As a result, every voice, every emotion, every thought you hear in your head is so loud that it drowns out the quieter, deeper voice of your soul. The only way to hear that voice is to turn off the ego, which you'll learn how to do momentarily.

Monster Attack

The ego, like all fairytale monsters, wants to devour you and make you its own. This monster is both patient and devious. It doesn't try to overwhelm you. If it did, you'd quickly catch on and recognize it for what it is. Instead, it has to be clever. It pulls you along, feeding you momentary pleasure every step of the way. It continually offers up temporary rewards so you'll fall prey to the illusion that your egocentric behavior is paying off. It feels good to go along with ego. Then, when you least expect it, your ego owns you. This could take years, even decades. But, because *time* has separated your egocentric deeds from their consequences, when chaos does come crashing down upon you, you don't think to connect the pain and turmoil to your previous behavior.

Time Is a Culprit

Time separates cause from effect. Time is the space between action and reaction. It is the delay between crime and consequence. The monster loves to use time to confuse you by making life appear random and chaotic. You see, you have a short memory. If you plant a negative seed today and the negative fruit of your action appears ten years down the line, the passage of time causes you to forget all about the seed. The negative fruit seems to be a sudden and random event. If you could see the relationship between cause and effect, action and reaction, chaos would suddenly turn into order. So the monster injects you with a shot of pleasure every time you respond to his suggestions, and then he *delays* the payback, creating the illusion of sudden chaos. In truth, there's an underlying order beneath all the turmoil. It's an utterly brilliant strategy!

(By the way, the monster may be implanting a bit of doubt in your mind this very moment; he doesn't want to let go of his iron-grip control over your life.)

The Payback

The pain and chaos that ensue as a result of ego come in different forms, including:

- Financial strife

- Marital and family strife

- Physical ailments

- Mental ailments

For instance, egocentric behavior in business might make you a fortune, but the payback can appear in your arteries (physical ailments) or in your relationship with your children or spouse (marital and family strife). Egocentric behavior with your friends and family might make you the center of attention, but the payback might be a downturn in business or an unhappy career (financial strife). This book happens to be about fears, so we'll focus on how the monster inflicts retribution in the area of mental ailments, which include all those needless fears and phobias.

To fully understand the role ego plays in all of this, you must first understand *why* ego exists and why you, a soul of humanity, wanted to have this monster infused into your very nature in the first place.

THE MONSTER IS CREATED

People didn't always have egos. They didn't always have fears. In fact, there was once a time and a place where people felt as fearless as superheroes, as secure as babies sleeping blissfully in the loving arms of their mothers. When and where did this fearless, monster-less existence exist? And what happened to it?

This wondrous realm of paradise existed *before* the physical world came into existence. Before Jesus. Before Muhammad. Before Moses. Even before Adam and Eve. It was a spiritual realm that was far more authentic and real than the physical world you now perceive with your five senses. It was the place from which all human souls originated.

Why don't you remember it? Why all the anxiety now? Why all the phobias? Why all the fright, panic attacks, and fear? Why has your ego been given full control over your life?

The answers to these basic questions of human existence have remained hidden away in the ancient teachings of Kabbalah for millennia. It's funny, because most
religions have told you how to live and behave. But
when you ask *why* the world came into being, and what
existed before the creation of the universe, they don't
provide much in the way of answers.

By contrast, the kabbalists of antiquity wrote more than
23 volumes dedicated to the subject of creation and
why human beings came into physical existence.
Obviously, I cannot present all that information in this
book, but I can condense that wisdom into a few key
points in order to explain where fears come from.
Understanding these cosmic secrets is the key. Not
only does this wisdom give you greater insights into the
dynamics of fear so you have the tools to rid yourself of
it, but the wisdom *itself* purifies you and washes away
fear as well. This latter point is important and worth
repeating: The kabbalistic wisdom concerning your ori-
gins and the meaning of life also serves to wash away
your fears and phobias.

Now let's discover why the universe was created.

CREATION IN A NUTSHELL

- The force called the Creator is an infinite force of energy. Kabbalah calls this force the Light.

- The Light is made up of endless happiness and joy.

- The Light wants only to share this happiness. The Light created the souls of humanity in order to share its endless joy.

- When souls were first created, they existed in a realm that predated the physical universe.

- This realm was filled with happiness and endless bliss, but the souls yearned for one more thing: They wanted to have a hand in *creating* their own bliss—just like their Creator—instead of having paradise handed to them like a free lunch. Just as a small child wants to grow up to become a self-sufficient adult like his or her own parents, the souls wanted to grow up to become creators like their Creator.

- So the Light hid itself, creating a tiny space of darkness where souls could assume a bodily form and create their own happiness. This microscopic space of darkness is our universe. Consider it boot camp, where souls train to become creators.

- Boot camp works like this: Human beings reveal the hidden Light and create their own happiness each time they share with another soul. This is what gives life meaning. This is how souls become creators of their own bliss, which is why they came here in the first place. This sounds simple, but it's not, for the following reasons:

  - To make the act of sharing a genuine accomplishment, the souls needed an opponent to test and challenge them. Imagine soccer players taking practice shots on an empty net. It's a worthless exercise. There must be a goalkeeper challenging them if their skill is going to develop. So the souls asked the Creator to create a challenger for them so they could develop the skill of sharing. This is the monster (the ego), whose only mission is to stop the souls from sharing with other human beings. Instead of thinking about others, the souls turn to their egos, which think only of themselves.

• Knowledge of the existence of the monster and the purpose of life, as described above, was hidden away in the recesses of the soul and the subconscious mind in order to make boot camp challenging. It is in your very nature to deny the ego's influence and to deny this very explanation of why the world exists. (By the way, you can also find

Light and reveal happiness when you reject
and overcome such denials.)

That's pretty much it, except for one more important
point. Reality has been set up according to the rules of
boot camp, meaning that it has been divided into two
distinct realms. As you are about to discover, the physical world is really just a blip on the screen of absolute
reality.

THE REALM OF FEAR

According to Kabbalah, reality is comprised of two distinct realms. First, there's the world you experience through your five senses. It's a place of sights, sounds, smells, tastes, and sensations. Unfortunately, it's also a world of darkness, danger, fear, and anxiety, with only occasional moments of happiness to break up the relentless tide of suffering.

This first realm is actually an illusion—it represents only 1% of true reality. Why is it an illusion? If you have a room lit up by a lamp, and you cover the lamp with a curtain, the room suddenly goes dark. The light is still shining. The light is still there. The darkness is merely an illusion created by the curtain. Lift it and the reality of the light is revealed.

This world is surrounded by a curtain. Let's take a peek behind it.

THE FEARLESS REALITY

According to Kabbalah, there's another reality, far more authentic and real than this one, but it's hidden behind a curtain. It's called the 99% Reality for the simple reason that 99% of existence is found there.

Whenever you experience happiness in any form, it means your soul has made contact with this hidden realm. Every invention, discovery, and advancement in human history occurred when people like Einstein, Newton, and Shakespeare logged into this unseen reality. Every time you feel joy, or experience a moment of insight, you are connecting to it. Whenever you feel the flow of happiness in your life, it means somehow you've tapped into this hidden 99% existence. Intuition, a "sixth sense," and "gut instincts" are all examples of dialing into this unseen reality. When people perform feats that are considered impossible in order to help another human being, they've made contact with the 99% Reality.

And guess what? There's no fear in the 99% Reality. There's nothing dark or dangerous there. Rather, it's a realm of pure Light, delight, contentment, power, wisdom, and joy—where all this is available in endless amounts. You might think of this as the Fearless Reality.

Fear and fearlessness work as follows:

- **You experience fear whenever you're separated from the 99% Reality.**

- **You experience fulfillment and fearlessness when you're close to and connected to this realm.**

The greater your separation from the 99% Reality, the more fear you experience.

The closer you are to this hidden realm, the greater the happiness and power you have in your life.

Separation Anxiety

Only one thing causes and increases your separation from the 99% Realm: *the monster*. The monster is the curtain that hides you from the Light, that covers the part of you that truly wants to share with other people. The monster is also a drapery manufacturer who *creates a new curtain every time you react to the orders he barks at you.*

Each new curtain dims the Light of the 99% Reality. Each new curtain creates greater separation between you and this radiant realm. Each new curtain increases darkness, *and within this darkness fear is born*. Just as the darkness caused by a curtain covering a lamp is an illusion, the darkness of fear is also an illusion, caused and maintained by the curtains that dim the Fearless Reality of the 99%.

THE **MONSTER** IS REAL

THE MONSTER IS REAL, THE FEAR IS NOT

"Pay no attention to the man behind the curtain!"
     —Wizard of Oz

Often in life we learn our greatest lessons through the power of story. The classic film *The Wizard of Oz* contains one such powerful story, along with a message about overcoming fear. Here's brief recap of the film:

> *Dorothy is a young girl from Kansas whose house is lifted up by a powerful tornado and transported to a strange world called Oz. Dorothy desperately wants to return home— especially when she finds that a wicked witch is after her. Luckily for Dorothy, Oz also has the support of good witches, including Glinda, who tells Dorothy that the great and powerful wizard of Oz might be able to help her get back to Kansas. Dorothy embarks on a journey fraught with danger to find him.*

Along the way, she befriends a scarecrow, a tin man, and a cowardly lion (no subtlety there). When the foursome finally confront the mysterious wizard, they are frightened out of their wits. The wizard has a booming voice and a giant ominous face, and smoke and lightning swirl all around him. But, as Dorothy's dog Toto discovers, the wizard is nothing but a little old man behind a curtain, fabricating the illusion of a terrifying wizard.

When the old man is exposed, he yells, "Pay no attention to that man behind the curtain!" But it's too late. Dorothy has uncovered the fraud.

Let's stop here for a moment and see how this story relates to what you've learned so far. Dorothy's childhood home of Kansas is the 99% Reality. Oz is the physical world, which includes both good witches and bad witches. The man behind the curtain is the ego, which constantly tells you to pay no attention to it, and you listen. Instead, you focus on the smoke and mirrors, bringing fear into your life. Make no mistake, the ego is a master illusionist, and its secret is hidden inside the very word that gives it power.

FEAR: False Evidence Appearing Real.

The first fear you must overcome is the fear of admitting the existence of your ego. That's right. Admitting and accepting the fact that your ego controls you is the first step in freeing yourself from your fears. Make no mistake, this is more difficult than you might imagine. The man behind the curtain works hard to make that task frightfully scary. In other words, you're afraid of exposing your ego to yourself and to others. You're scared to death of admitting that you're an egocentric being. If you strike your ego down to real size, you'll become more vulnerable. You're afraid that people will now hurt, abuse, or make fun of you. Without your ego, you're afraid that you'll attain less from life, so you hang onto your ego for dear life. You can't pry yourself loose. But the fear is an illusion. It's all smoke and mirrors. In fact, the smoke and mirrors are so real, you don't even realize that you have an ego most of the time.

However, the moment you can admit to yourself—and to others—that *all* your behavior is controlled by your ego, you have just pulled a "Toto" and exposed the man behind the curtain. Now you're ready for the next step. Let's return to our adventure in Oz and find out what that next step is.

> *Dorothy uncovers the real man behind the curtain, who tells her what she must do to get back home: She must confront the wicked witch and retrieve her broomstick. Terrified, Dorothy and her friends nevertheless head straight to the witch's castle, where they confront her. The witch ignites her broomstick and uses it to set the scarecrow on fire. At that moment, Dorothy puts all her fears aside and goes to the rescue of her beloved friend. She pours water on the scarecrow and douses the flames. When some of the water spills*

*onto the wicked witch, the terrifying old dame
instantly melts away.*

Think about this. How does Dorothy wind up defeating
her wicked adversary? She does it through a simple act
of sharing. Dorothy forgets about herself and helps the
scarecrow. When you confront your fears and engage in
acts of sharing, your own terrors will melt away as well.

*Upon defeating the witch, Dorothy returns to
the wizard and he reveals a wondrous secret.
The power to return home is already within
Dorothy. It always has been. With three clicks
of her heels, she is transported out of the illusion of Oz and back into her bed in Kansas,
surrounded by her loved ones.*

Once you defeat a particular fear, the power to return
home to the 99% Realm of Light is awakened within
you. You always have that power. You just have to
defeat fear in order to awaken it. When you do, your

soul connects to your home and Light flows to you in the here and now.

Before you learn how to accomplish all of this in more detail, let's first examine the kinds of fears that torment you, and expose them for what they truly are.

Part Two

COMPREHEND-ING AND CONQUERING FEAR

WHAT IS FEAR?

You know what fear is, or you think you do. It happens when you perceive a threat (real or imagined). On a physical level, you go into emergency mode; your body releases a torrent of chemicals as the "fight-or-flight" response kicks in.

Originally discovered by renowned Harvard physiologist Walter Cannon, the fight-or-flight response is instinctual.

- **"Fight" means your body braces for battle.**

- **"Flight" means you prepare to flee from danger.**

Both actions set off the same bodily responses. Your adrenaline pumps. Your respiratory rate increases. Cortisol is released. Blood is directed away from your digestive tract to your muscles and limbs. Your pupils dilate. Your sense of danger is heightened. Rational thinking goes out the window.

This was all very helpful many years ago when a hungry lion was roaring from a nearby thicket. Today it can be unhealthy when this response kicks in every time you step into a crowded elevator, or your boss yells at you, or your mother-in-law gets on the phone. Constant fight-or-fight response means chronic stress, which can lead to all sorts of problems, including fatigue, depression, headaches, and a weakened immune system. In this state, you're always reacting and your life seems to be spinning into chaos—which is just the opposite of what you want.

A Mirage

On a psychological level, fear creates an imaginary future that doesn't really exist. For example, you fear that flying may lead to a plane crash, so you avoid the thing you fear (by driving instead). Usually the bad thing hasn't actually happened to you, and probably never will. This can be true for anything, from asking someone on a date, to speaking in public, to walking on a quiet street late at night.

Before learning how to deal with your fears, it's important to realize that needless fear comes in two strengths: anxiety (regular) and phobia (extrastrength).

Anxiety

A little anxiety, or a small dose of fear, can be healthy. Normal anxiety can help you prepare for an uncomfortable situation, such as speaking in public, asking your boss for a raise, or speaking to an employee about the pink slip you're about to hand him or her. A fear of running blindfolded across a busy intersection is a healthy fear. A fear of hurting other people can also be a healthy fear. If a smoke alarm goes off in your house, the surge of adrenaline you experience is a good thing. But if the fire alarm is malfunctioning and goes off incessantly, all those false alarms create havoc in your life. You keep urgently reacting to nothing! And if your fear of public speaking or just speaking your mind to a friend keeps you from stepping up to the podium or having that difficult let's-clear-the-air conversation, then that fear no longer serves you.

THE **MONSTER** IS REAL

The monster inside of you loves to have you react to unhealthy fears. He encourages you to worry and fret all day long, and he's very effective. According to a study conducted by the University of Pennsylvania, Americans devote one to eight hours a day to worrying. This study included a number of other interesting results:

- 40% of the worries never materialized.

- 30% of the worries were about the past, where absolutely nothing could be done about them.

- 12% of the worries were directed toward other people's business.

- 10% of the worries were spent on real or imaginary illnesses.

- Only 8% of the worries were justified.

Extreme Anxiety

Extreme forms of anxiety (anxiety disorders) are often triggered by such potentially difficult issues as money, family, health, and relationships with friends and partners. Once again, the smoke alarm keeps going off even though there's no smoke; you find yourself always expecting the worst, anticipating disaster even though you realize there's little basis for it. When you experience extreme anxiety, it's hard to relax and it's difficult to fall asleep or remain asleep throughout the night. You might feel dizzy or experience difficulty breathing. Some people get nauseous or sweaty, and then become more anxious about embarrassing themselves in front of others. That thought arouses even more anxiety, creating a vicious circle.

Panic Attacks

Panic attacks seem to come out of nowhere and they can hit you with overwhelming force. Instead of having a simple, battery-operated smoke alarm going off in your house, now you hear a four-alarm fire bell accompanied by sirens, people shouting in fear, and the roaring engines of speeding fire trucks.

Symptoms can include shortness of breath, dizziness, and feelings of dread and doom. Your hands might tingle or get cold. Your breathing can become shallow. You might feel like you have to fight for air. Your heart can pound like a tribal drum. You might think you're having a heart attack. Some people feel like they're losing touch with reality.

Panic can paralyze you. It can stop you from getting onto an airplane or even from leaving the safe confines of your home. The problem can then be compounded by negative thoughts about the attack itself. You begin to believe that something's really wrong with you. You start devising all kinds of dreadful scenarios in your mind. This feeds the anxiety, which in turn feeds the physiological responses that heighten the panic, and the vicious cycle builds on itself.

Kabbalistically, a panic attack is caused by the monster. He has access to ego-driven thoughts that shift your body's physiology into panic mode. He can flood your mind with visions of doom and feelings of terror. He can jump-start your flow of adrenaline so your racing heart validates your irrational worries. This triggers even more adrenaline, and once again you're in a spiraling circle of panic. Negative emotions and worries and all the negative bodily responses are incited by the monster through the power you give him each time you react.

Phobias

A phobia is like anxiety on steroids. While a little anxiety can be good for you, phobias have no upside at all. Anxieties can vary from mild to extreme, and they can be either general ("What if something goes wrong today at work?") or specific ("What if I try to deliver today's presentation and make a mess of it?"). Phobias, on the other hand, are both intense and specific, such as fear of spiders (arachnophobia), fear of tight quarters (claustrophobia), or fear of flying (aviophobia). These are extreme anxieties—dominating and irrational fears of something very specific. A phobia holds you back from taking actions you want or need to take; it blocks you from experiencing the rewards of those actions and from taking the next steps in life.

While anxieties influence decisions and behavior, phobias control them. A person with arachnophobia won't enter a room with a spider, no matter what. If there's a spider in the hallway and the person wants to go outside, he'll climb through a window rather than step into the hallway leading to the door. If the only way out is through the hallway, he won't go out at all. He could be invited to dinner with the president of the United States tonight, or getting married in an hour, but as long as that spider remains in the hallway, he'll stay inside, paralyzed by fear. This may sound silly, but anyone who's had firsthand experience with the power of phobias, anxiety attacks, or panic attacks knows that in those moments the fearful grip of illusion is all-consuming.

TWO RESPONSES TO THE MONSTER

Whether you're dealing with selfishness, fear, greed, anger, or any other destructive impulse dictated by your ego, you have two choices as to how to respond.

1. You can react, and behave according to the monster's wishes.

2. You can resist the monster and stop your reactions dead in their tracks.

If you choose the latter, you replace being reactive with being proactive.

For the record:

> Every time you put yourself into a proactive state, it is considered an act of sharing.

Therein lies the key secret to ending your fears. When you react, you're sharing with absolutely no one. Your anger, fear, jealousy, and envy negatively affect a human being, either directly or indirectly, either yourself or someone else.

However, when you resist the desire to react and you shut off the radio broadcasting those monster hits, you are now being proactive. Everyone around you benefits from your behavior, so you are clearly sharing. And that, my friend, means you've just torn down a curtain, allowing the Light of the 99% Reality to shine brighter in your life. When there's more Light in your life, there's less darkness and less fear.

REACTIONS ARE THE ROOT

The monster is all about getting you to react—*to anything!*

Why?

Each time you react, you feed the monster. The Light grows dimmer. Life gets darker. The monster grows stronger. Now the monster can use that added darkness to fabricate new illusions of fear in order to stimulate even more reactions within you.

Reactions are the key to his power. Therefore:

- If someone insults you, the monster incites the reaction of anger or hurt.

- If someone makes more money than you, the monster incites the reaction of envy.

THE **MONSTER** IS REAL 61

- If someone pays you a nice compliment, the monster incites the reaction of being flattered by the praise.

How Fears Are Manufactured

Small reactions in your life erect small curtains. These small curtains cause a little bit of darkness, which manifests as new, small fears. (These bits of darkness can also manifest as spats with your spouse, annoying financial difficulties, or minor health issues. The monster decides which kind of chaos will be part of your life, but since this book is about fear, our focus will remain on that.) Big, ongoing reactions in your life erect bigger curtains, which lead to greater darkness and a larger number of fears of greater intensity.

This is how fears are born. Every time you react in life, whether it's justified or not, the monster hangs up a curtain. Don't let the monster implant doubts about this fact in your mind, which he is probably trying to do right about now. *Pay attention* to the monster behind the curtain and you can begin to cut down on the reactions he constantly incites within you.

Here are some more examples of the monster at work:

- You react with anger when family members annoy you.

- You react with jealousy when friends or business colleagues achieve a little more success than you do.

- You react with impatience when the driver of the car in front of you drives too slowly or takes too long to make that left-hand turn.

- You react with a desire for vengeance when your enemies inflict chaos in your life.

Once a reaction has taken place and you've hurt someone else (even if they deserved it), you now have a

THE **MONSTER** IS REAL

situation that needs to be corrected. Let's call this a *reaction infraction*.

There Is No Right or Wrong

Reaction infractions are the root cause of fears. Each reaction infraction erects a curtain that creates darkness into which fears are born. It's that simple. If you want to start banishing fears from your life, you have to go back to the root and repair a past reaction, *even if you're sure your reaction was warranted.*

You see, life is *not* about who's right and who's wrong. Life is *only* about becoming the creator of your own fulfillment by finding the hidden Light. *You do that each time you share with someone.* That's the rule of the game. If someone wrongs you, and you react, you aren't sharing. You might be right, but you also just hung up a curtain in the process. That's what nobody in this world seems to understand. They haven't figured that one out yet. And that's why the world abounds in sorrow and pain. Ask yourself this: Would you rather be right—*and miserable?* Or would you rather be wrong—*and happy?*

Make no mistake: *Right does not make Light.*

On the contrary, sharing makes Light. You share when you're proactive toward the people and events in your life. You become proactive when you shut down the monster and the reactions he triggers.

CORRECTING THE ROOT, BANISHING THE FEAR

According to Kabbalah, there's only one way to correct a reaction infraction and the word *sorry* has nothing to do with it. Saying you're sorry does not remove the other person's pain. Being sorry does not prevent you from having the same reaction again under different circumstances a week or two later. To correct a reaction infraction, you must:

> **Eradicate the trait inside yourself that caused you to react in the first place.**

In other words, you must destroy a little bit of the monster within you. You must recognize, admit, and acknowledge those ugly little traits that live within you, no matter how scary the prospect might be. Once you overcome the fear of acknowledging your ego, then you go to the next phase, which is to work very hard at eliminating those ego traits from your nature.

Fortunately, the universe has been set up so that life will send you all the opportunities you'll ever need to destroy those monster traits inside yourself.

And as you'll soon see, that's what fear is all about! Fear gives you an opportunity to banish the reactive traits within your nature that caused the fear in the first place.

Before you learn how to correct a reaction infraction and banish the fear, let's examine the relationship between your fears and your reactions.

HOW PARTICULAR FEARS MATERIALIZE

Suppose your reactions in life are primarily related to control issues. For example, the monster causes you to manipulate people, argue with colleagues, and even tell white lies to your friends, just so you can maintain a sense of control over various situations and relationships. If your reactions center on issues of control, so will your fears.

For instance, fear of flying is often related to fear of having no control. If you knew you had the ability to safely land the plane at a moment's notice, your fear of flying would vanish.

Suppose you're a controlling person and your job is to manage a sales force. One of your salespeople has a suggestion for improving sales, and she'd like to present it to the president of the company. You react. You want to control the situation. You feel insecure about relinquishing control to the rep and having her talk directly to the president, so you refuse to allow her to present the idea. Instead, you present it on her behalf. Now she's hurt by your lack of trust in her loyalty (hurting someone is not sharing with someone), and you have a reactive situation in need of repair.

Reactions over control issues might very well contribute to fears like claustrophobia. You might feel trapped in small quarters, panicky that you can't escape, but if you knew you had the control to leave the room whenever you felt like it, the fear would vanish. It's about control.

You might be a person who abuses others with your speech . You monopolize conversations. You speak because you enjoy hearing yourself talk. You constantly disregard the opinions of those around you. You have a rough day at work and you lash out at your spouse when you get home. Reactions like those can lead to fears associated with speaking. For instance, you might have a terrible fear of public speaking. Or a fear of speaking your mind to your boss or employees. Or you're always terrified of saying the wrong thing. Your reactions and your fears are closely related.

When Blood Flows

In Kabbalah, there's a form of wrongdoing that's referred to as bloodshed. Naturally, this includes physical violence. But the kabbalists told us 2,000 years ago that the *crime of bloodshed* also refers to shaming someone in private or public, causing their face to turn red out of embarrassment. Humiliation is akin to spilling a person's blood.

If someone really angers you during an argument and the monster incites you to respond by embarrassing him or her with a clever comeback line, that reaction hangs up a curtain. Life gets a little bit darker. A fear, relating to the flow of blood, now awaits you. This might take the form of an anxiety attack, which causes your heart to start beating a mile a minute, or your face to become flushed, hot, and sweaty.

Thou Shall Not Kill

Consider the sin of murder. You can assassinate a person with a bullet, or you can commit character assassination by spreading gossip or talking negatively behind a person's back. One kills the body; the other kills the soul. Such reaction infractions lead to fears such as panic attacks, where you feel like you're dying. Or you experience chest pains or difficulty breathing. Or you may be afflicted with an overwhelming fear of death.

Your reactions determine the kinds of fear that will come back into your life. All the while, the monster is blinding you to the truth of his existence inside you.

On the surface, the preceding examples make it seem as though fears are some kind of payback, as if phobias are really a form of retribution.

Not at all. On the contrary.

FEARS ARE NOT PUNISHMENTS

Fears are opportunities, not punishments. They offer you a possibility, not a penalty. How? They provide you with an *opportunity* to correct a previous reactive infraction. They extend to you the *possibility* of fixing something in your past.

The following story will help you understand how.

> *MAX, THE MESSAGE, AND THE FLOOD*
> *In a small village not so long ago, a terrible rainstorm struck. It rained so hard, for so long, that the entire village was quickly becoming a flood zone. Max, the village carpenter, stood on his porch looking incredulously at the rising waters. Suddenly, the sheriff of the village pulled up in a jeep. "Max, you have to hurry," the sheriff yelled. "We need to evacuate. Jump in my car and I'll drive you to safety."*

Max stood on his porch. He stared up into the sky. Then he looked at the sheriff. "I have trust in God, sheriff. He'll save me. I'm staying right here." The sheriff pleaded with Max, but it was no use.

An hour later the waters had completely covered the street and Max's property. Suddenly, a man in a boat spotted Max and pulled up to the porch. "Mister, climb aboard," the man called out. "This rain is not going to stop for days."

Max stood his ground. "No thank you," he said. "I have trust and faith in God. He'll rescue me. I'm not going to panic." The boat then motored off.

Meanwhile, the waters had now reached Max's waist. Suddenly, a helicopter hovered over Max's house. A rope ladder was dropped. It fell directly in front of Max.

"Grab a hold of the ladder and we'll you bring up," screamed the pilot. To which Max responded, *"I'm staying right here. God will save me."* The helicopter flew away and the rain kept coming. The water had now reached Max's neck. Then his mouth. Then his nostrils. Max drowned.

Up in heaven, Max was walking around utterly confused. He asked if he could have an appointment with God. His request was granted, and Max met with the Creator of the universe.

"With all due respect, my Heavenly Father, I don't understand what happened on earth. I stood on my porch waiting for you, showing utter conviction and faith in your ability to save me. What happened?"

God shook His head. *"What are you talking about, Max?"* He asked. *"I sent you a jeep, a boat, and a helicopter! What more could you ask?"*

The Light works through people and situations. Help comes to you in many ways, but you don't recognize it most of the time. Fears are there to help you. They're messages sent to you so you can fix reactive behavior from your past. This removes the curtains that have darkened your life so you can become the creator of Light and happiness in your life. From this perspective, fears are actually a tool to help you achieve happiness. You used to run away from them. *Now you know you should seek them out.*

Seek them out? Absolutely yes! Fears give you an opportunity to wipe out the trait that caused you to react in the first place. That's why fear happens. On the other side of the fear is Light. So when a fear strikes, it means *Light is also waiting for you.* How do you get past the fear and reach the Light? You do it in two ways:

1. **You accept responsibility for the fear, *knowing* that it's the effect of a reactive trait within you.**

2. **You face the fear and overcome it, *knowing* that the pain of the fear and the conquering of it will weaken the reactive trait and thus destroy a little bit of the monster.**

This is the key. This is how you gradually eliminate fears from your life. Accepting responsibility and being willing to endure some pain in order to get closer to the Light is the magic formula for making your fears evaporate.

This is what I was referring to earlier when I said that kabbalistic wisdom, in and of itself, helps wash away your fears. It's a great example of the power and role of human consciousness and knowledge. If you experience a fear without understanding why it exists, all your pain will be for nothing. Even if you overcome a fear in a specific circumstance, the fear will still return. *Knowledge* is the key to removing the root of the fear completely. Knowledge as to why it exists and its connection to the meaning of life is the weapon that uproots all fear at the seed level. Let's examine this idea further.

Why Knowledge Is the Key

This secret about the power of knowledge is found in a strikingly odd biblical verse that has confounded scholars, rabbis, priests, and popes for thousands of years, even to this very day. The verse concerns Adam, Eve, and the birth of Cain. Found in Genesis, it states:

Adam knew Eve, his wife, and she bore Cain.

Kabbalah asks the question: Why does The Bible use the word *knew* to imply a sexual connection between a man and a woman? Why not use the words *intercourse* or *sexual relations* to convey the same idea? Think about it. When was the last time a woman became pregnant simply by knowing a man?

Kabbalists tell us that this unusual biblical verse is actually code.

Let's decipher it:

- *Adam* is a code for the 99% Realm, the Fearless Reality.

- *Eve* is a code for our physical world, the 1% Realm of fears.

- *Knew* is a code referring to the concept of knowledge.

Now follow this next idea closely: When you want to connect the two worlds so Light flows into your life, you must possess kabbalistic knowledge as to how and why things work in the physical and spiritual realms. In other words, *knowledge* is how you make a connection to the 99%. According to Kabbalah, blind faith or the wrong information in life will always keep you in the dark. But correct knowledge connects you to Light.

Intercourse between the 1% and the 99% takes place only when knowledge is in your consciousness. In other words:

- You have to *know* about the existence of the 99% in order to connect to it.

- You have to *know* about the curtain that hides the Light and causes your fear in order to be able to connect to the curtain and tear it down.

- You have *know* that you're responsible for your fear because of your past reactive behavior in order to connect to its original cause and eradicate it.

- You have to *know* about the existence of the ego/monster in order to connect to it and destroy it.

Prior to reading this book, you probably never knew that any of the above even existed. Now you do. And now you'll immediately feel a deeper sense of security, power, and courage in your life. You'll feel a huge difference and improvement in respect to your fears, just from this basic understanding of how life works. In fact, I know people whose fears vanished just from taking one class on Kabbalah that explored the preceding ideas. Never underestimate the power of kabbalistic knowledge. It's not like learning math or history, which make you wiser but are still just information. Kabbalistic knowledge is the actual Light itself. Thus, when that knowledge/Light becomes part of your being, part of your essence, there's less darkness inside you. *And that means less fear.*

Consider the case of a student I'll call Robert. Robert was agoraphobic; he had a fear of the outdoors, of leaving home. He explains how the wisdom of Kabbalah helped him overcome a particular fear:

> *My agoraphobia had reached the point where*
> *I couldn't even go to the corner store to buy*
> *milk without experiencing the worst feeling of*

panic you can imagine. I could hardly breathe when I was in the store. Only when I got back into my car and started driving home did the panic subside. I couldn't go into a shopping mall because I didn't want to be too far from the exit and my car.

Once, I had to drive with my wife to visit her parents. They lived about an hour from our home. Halfway there, I broke out in a terrible sweat. I was hyperventilating. Each second that the car sped along the highway, farther from my house, my panic intensified. My wife looked at me like I was nuts. My face was covered in sweat and I was too paralyzed with fear to wipe the sweat away. Finally, I pulled off the highway and headed back home.

The shame I felt was terrible. I couldn't believe I let this rotten fear control my life. There were some months when I was strong and could cope with it. Other months I couldn't

even leave the house. Anyway, a few years later I came across Kabbalah. I began studying and was blown away by the wisdom. Just knowing that the 99% existed gave me great comfort and hope.

One time, my Kabbalah teacher told me to drive to New York to attend a special Kabbalistic event. It was about a ten-hour drive, and I was freaked out by the prospect. But then I said to myself, "If the Light is real, if the 99% Realm truly exists and I break my nature by accepting responsibility for the fear, nothing can happen." I knew, based on what I'd learned, that overcoming the fear would fix my previous reactive moments. So I agreed.

We packed our car and drove off to New York, and I didn't have a single panic attack. It's hard to explain. It wasn't like I was using some kind of kabbalistic tool (which, of course, there are many) to help me cope. It was just a general feeling of calm and certainty. In other words, instead of driving or flying somewhere for business and money or for a vacation, I knew I was now traveling to help further my connection to the Light. This just filled me with a sense of serenity and goodness. The concepts and the principles of Kabbalah had always filled me with this feeling of goodness. I guess panic and serenity can't exist at the same time.

Over the years, as I learned and practiced more, I utilized the wisdom AND the tools to completely eradicate my fears. But the point of this story is to tell you that, at the very beginning of my involvement with Kabbalah, I achieved a measure of relief from panic, even before I began using all the tools.

I'll repeat the technique for conquering a fear:

1. **You accept responsibility for the fear, *knowing* that it's the effect of a reactive trait within you.**

2. **You face the fear and overcome it, *knowing* that the pain of the fear and the conquering of it will weaken the reactive trait and thus destroy a little bit of the monster.**

This technique is simple but it's not easy to do. The monster will crank up the fear inside you to try to prevent you from connecting to the Light. As you consider facing the fear, the monster arouses even greater fear. Unfortunately, most of the time, you give in to the illusions the monster creates.

When you're too afraid to confront your fear, then the reaction infraction (your original reactive behavior) still hangs over your head. The monster remains at large, which means you'll react again in the future. Not having been confronted, the monster grows stronger, meaning that more intense fears will plague you until you overcome the monster. Without this kabbalistic knowledge, you become more and more frightened, more panic stricken, more crippled by your fears. Now that you know what's really happening, the monster has been exposed. Now you have to expose him to the Light.

In our final section, we'll explore some techniques for triumphing over fear and living a life free of anxiety and panic.

Part Three

TECHNIQUES FOR OVER- COMING FEAR

Before we examine the specific techniques, here's a simple but powerful formula for confronting and conquering fear:

FORMULA FOR STRESS, ANXIETY, AND FEAR

1. **Identify the symptoms that are triggered by the stressful situation. Acknowledge the reason for the anxiety: *previous reactive behavior.***

2. **Move toward the stressful situation and prepare to confront it by resisting the fight-or-flight response, knowing it's the monster inciting your symptoms.**

3. **Gradually tolerate the feelings of discomfort by allowing the fear or anxiety to get stronger. Acknowledge that the pain is eliminating your reactive trait. This will make you a more sharing person.**

4. **Confront the fear with certainty and trust, knowing that freedom and happiness await you on the other side.**

TECHNIQUE #1: THE ART OF SHARING

The purpose of life, as you've learned, is for you to create your own happiness and Light. You do this a little bit each time you share.

One way to deal with a moment of fear and anxiety is to shift into sharing mode the moment fear strikes. Look for someone to help. Take an action outside yourself. According to Kabbalah, when you find yourself gripped by fear and anxiety, you're thinking only about yourself. Reactive behavior distances you from the 99%, so perform a sharing action. Sharing connects you to the 99%. Automatically, the Light that flows from this realm displaces your fear just as a light bulb displaces darkness from a room.

A good friend of mine had a terrible fear of flying. He used this technique to help him overcome a frightening situation. Here's the story in his own words:

SHARING AT 30,000 FEET

I hate to fly, but when I do, I feel more comfortable on a large aircraft where I don't feel so claustrophobic. One day I was forced to fly on a private jet for an important business meeting. We had to fly from New York to Wisconsin, and on the way back we had to stop in Virginia to drop off two passengers. There were five of us on the plane, and I had to hide my fear of flying so I wouldn't look like an idiot in front of my associates.

During the flight to Wisconsin I did some kabbalistic meditation on The Zohar, the major book of Kabbalah, and I felt good. After the meeting, we boarded the plane and headed for Virginia. Again I meditated on The Zohar to help me overcome the fears. We dropped off our passengers in Roanoke and were on our way back to New York. By this time, I started feeling very relaxed because the majority of the air travel was over.

Then it happened. We were halfway to New York when the copilot came out of the cockpit and said we weren't being allowed to land. Air traffic controllers hadn't given him a reason, and he looked worried. He said that in all his years of flying, he had never not been given a reason. He said it was probably a terrorist alert and air traffic control probably didn't want to cause alarm. My heart started pounding. My breathing became shallow. Then the pilot said we didn't have enough fuel to circle around waiting for clearance, so he would phone the charter company and see where we could go for fuel. I looked out the window and was flooded with claustrophobic thoughts of being trapped in this plane. I reminded myself that these worries were not real, and that they were only the monster inside me arousing my fear.

The pilot then discovered that the satellite phone was broken. He had no way to call out, and now he was getting really flustered. I began worrying about running out of gas 30,000 feet up in the sky. The copilot got down on his hands and knees and started frantically trying to repair the phone. It looked like a scene out of a movie.

I opened up The Zohar again and started meditating even harder. One of my friends in the plane ordered a vodka from the flight attendant. The other associate lit up a joint, and the cabin filled with the smell of marijuana. I had to admit to myself, even in the midst of my fear, that it was a funny scene. Suddenly one of my friends jumped up and said he couldn't find his luggage in the back of the plane. He started freaking out. He said somebody in Virginia probably took his luggage by accident, and he had very important documents inside it. Meanwhile, the copilot was still on his hands and knees, trying to fix the phone.

At that moment I realized something pro-found. If I kept meditating to make myself feel better, I was still being reactive; I was thinking only about myself and that would only fuel more fears. I saw how upset my friend was over his missing luggage. Then I realized that I could use my cell phone and call the people we'd dropped off in Virginia.

I have to tell you, my fear at that moment was paralyzing, but I figured either Kabbalah works or it doesn't. I was taught that when you find yourself in the grip of fear, share. So I did. I put The Zohar away. I pulled out my phone and started dialing. Suddenly, I felt a profound sense of calm and certainty. I felt as though I was in total control of the plane and my consciousness would control everything that happened next. I called the people in Virginia and, sure enough, they had the lug-gage. My friend on the plane was so relieved. Suddenly, the satellite phone worked. The

THE **MONSTER** IS REAL

copilot told the charter company that we'd fly back to Virginia to refuel, since we also had to pick up the missing luggage. I was blissfully calm.

As we landed in Virginia to pick up the luggage, the airport in New York cleared us to return. We were told that we'd been rerouted due to a sudden thunderstorm, which had passed. The flight back to New York was perfect.

A great Kabbalist once said, "When you get busy worrying about the welfare of others, the Light gets busy worrying about you."

TECHNIQUE #2:
THE WILLINGNESS FACTOR

According to an ancient military saying, *If you would have peace, prepare for war.* An enemy who sees that you're prepared to fight a war is unlikely to start one. The same logic applies to confronting your fears. This is the second technique: If you're fully prepared to confront your fears—really, truly prepared and determined to do so—events often arrange themselves in such a way that the confrontation never takes place. Remember, the goal (both yours and the Light's) is to effect genuine change within yourself; the fear is just a trigger to help incite the change.

A classic example of this may be found in the old kabbalistic tale of a man who went to his teacher, a great Kabbalist, and confessed terrible wrongs. The Kabbalist told him that the things he had done were so bad that the only possible atonement in this life would be an agonizingly painful death, such as that caused by drinking mercury. After a period of soul searching, the man agreed and asked his master to administer the poison, since he wasn't sure he could do it himself. The Kabbalist told him to lie on his back on the floor, close his eyes, and hold his mouth open as long as possible. The man did as instructed, and the Kabbalist poured the glass of liquid down the man's throat. The liquid, however, was nothing more than cold water. The Kabbalist then explained to the man that he had clearly changed himself to the point where he was ready to die in order to atone for his crimes—and because of that, he didn't have to. He had faced the greatest fear of all, the fear of dying, and this action banished all the negative traits that had caused him to commit his misdeeds.

Always remember that *willingness* is 99% of the battle.

TECHNIQUE #3:
RITUALS OF LIGHT

Like it or not, you're a creature of habit. You can choose good habits or bad. Unfortunately, because the monster has been given control over the airwaves of your mind, bad habits are easy to pick up while good habits are harder to come by. It only takes a moment to get hooked on chocolate or crack cocaine; one taste can do it. But no one ever got hooked on daily exercise after just one workout.

The monster wants you to acquire bad habits. *All the time.* Each time you react, you strengthen him, and he now can inflict more intense reactions and thoughts upon you. You came to this world to make sharing second nature, but the monster has made selfishness your primary pattern. Each time you react and behave selfishly, you empower the monster further.

This is where Kabbalah parts ways with conventional psychotherapy treatments. Traditional self-help techniques accomplish just that—they help the self. And as you just learned, *the self is the monster!* The *true you* is your soul, the quiet voice and deep feelings that emanate from your innermost being. Instead of undergoing *self-help* treatments, you should be engaging in *help others* exercises.

Kabbalah's tools are designed to help you accomplish just that. These tools weaken the monster so you can become a more sharing and loving person. If you're like most people, you probably aren't motivated by morals, ethics, or lofty spiritual ideals, although they can certainly help. You share because sharing is how you draw more Light and happiness into your own life!

To help you break the stranglehold that the monster has over you, the ancient kabbalists provided some tools that help connect your soul to the 99% Reality. These tools can be used every day to infuse you with the Light. This Light weakens the monster, vanquishing the darkness and banishing the fears that lurk within you.

The 72 Names of God

God doesn't really have names or aliases, so the kabbalistic phrase *Names of God* is a code referring to spiritual forces that can help you in various areas of your life. For instance, there are Names of God that can be used to promote healing, provide prosperity, or remove fears. These Names were revealed in *The Zohar* some 2,000 years ago.

The Zohar was written in the ancient language of Aramaic, but that doesn't mean you need to know Aramaic or any other language to access the power of the Names. The simple fact of the matter is, the Names are actually meditative devices. You simply gaze at or meditate upon the shapes of the letters that compose a particular Name. When you make visual contact, energy flows from the 99% Reality into your soul by way of your eyes (long ago, kabbalists already knew that the eyes were the windows to the soul).

Here are three Names you can meditate upon every day to fill your being with Light and remove your fears.

Meditation upon a Name can consist of simply looking at the letters for a few moments, or you can spend five to ten minutes engaging in deep-breathing relaxation exercises as you meditate upon the Name. Both work. When you make meditation a daily habit, it will serve not just to remove your fears but also to enrich your entire life.

Utilize this Name to banish all obsessive, negative, and unwanted thoughts. .

Utilize this Name to *cure* your fears, not just cope with them.

עָרִי

Use this Name to give you 100% certainty in your ability to conquer any fearful situation, including the certainty that Light is waiting for you on the other side of fear.

The Zohar

The Zohar is another powerful tool for filling your entire being with Light. I know people all over the world who have used *The Zohar* to heal themselves of disease and cure themselves of even the most intense phobias and anxieties. Simply spend five minutes a day visually scanning the Aramaic text of *The Zohar*. The great kabbalists all agree that this seemingly unusual action is incredibly powerful. The moment your eyes make contact with the text, tremendous energy ignites. Don't let the monster tell you this is irrational. If you want to consider what's rational, never forget that unhealthy fear, extreme anxiety, and phobias are the most irrational

THE **MONSTER** IS REAL

things in the world. Just try it. If it works for you, keep using it.

The Zohar in Action

A certain student of Kabbalah had difficulty sleeping. He had a bad habit of waking up every night around 2:00 A.M., feeling anxious, and he couldn't fall back to sleep for hours. His mind raced through a litany of worries. One day, he had an idea. He understood that it was the monster who was waking him up and tormenting him with negative thoughts, so every time he woke up, he thanked himself (the monster) for waking himself and then he meditated upon *The Zohar*. He did this every night for a few nights. The monster began to realize that he was helping to develop a good habit, one that released tremendous Light, so he stopped and the man has been sleeping soundly ever since. That was over ten years ago.

Rituals of Darkness

Technique #3 also relates to a very powerful condition known as obsessive-compulsive disorder.

You now know that the monster bombards you with negative thoughts, and each time you react to people and events in your life, you make the monster stronger. If you keep reacting to everything in your life, the situation eventually gets out of hand as your reactive thoughts spin out of control. That leads to obsessive-compulsive disorder, or OCD.

Obsessive thoughts are repetitive and intrusive thoughts that cause you great discomfort. They can range from fear of germs to thoughts of evil actions, bizarre sexual thoughts, superstitious thoughts, and thoughts about hurting yourself or others. Obsessive thoughts are irrational, invasive, and recurring. OCD sufferers may find one of the following thoughts familiar:

- "My hands are dirty, I need to wash them again."

- "If I don't double-check all the locks in the house, a burglar might come."

- "If I shut the TV off on a certain channel or on a bad image, something bad will happen."

Obsessive-compulsive thoughts can also include endless doubts about safety issues, like worrying every single night that you forgot to shut off the oven.

Thoughts Are Harmless

According to Kabbalah, thoughts aren't dangerous. Why? Because thoughts don't originate from your soul. They're not you. They're merely implanted by the monster, the ego aspect of your nature. Most people, who lack kabbalistic insights, feel tremendous guilt and anxiety over obsessive thoughts. Once you know that those thoughts don't belong to you, you can drop the guilt and let go of the worry.

If, however, you take ownership of those thoughts and act upon them, they can become very harmful by leading to compulsive behavior.

Compulsion

When you listen to compulsive thoughts and perform repetitive actions and rituals, you engage in compulsive behavior. Compulsion leads people to avoid stepping on cracks on the sidewalk, or if they do, to back up and re-walk the same route. Some people change the channel on their TVs before going to bed until they find a program or commercial that doesn't make them feel uneasy. Others must constantly look over their shoulders whenever they walk through their neighborhoods.

A repetitive ritual can provide a temporary sense of relief from obsessive thoughts but, of course, it's a trap. The more you give in to the ritual, the stronger the compulsion becomes.

Creatures of Habit

Since habitual behavior is part of human nature, you're either going to develop rituals and routines that bring you Light (which is why the kabbalists designed rituals such as daily meditation on *The Zohar* and the Names of God) or you'll develop rituals that bring you darkness.

Kabbalistic rituals bring you Light that weakens the monster and strengthens your desire to share. The more you share, the more Light you receive and the happier you become.

Start developing positive rituals. These can include:

- Performing small or large acts of sharing every day—the kind of sharing that's uncomfortable to do

- Meditating daily upon the Names of God

- Meditating daily upon *The Zohar*.

- Recognizing and resisting at least one reaction every day

- Spending five minutes or an hour reading a book on the wisdom of Kabbalah

If you fail to make rituals of Light part of your daily routine, a void opens up in your life. The monster will compel you to fill that empty space with *his* rituals, which include obsessive-compulsive behavior. Instead of Light, you get darkness, and that means more fear. The bottom line is that habits and rituals that awaken Light prevent habits and rituals that create darkness.

As the Swiss philosopher Henri Frederic Amiel once wrote, "To learn new habits is everything, for it is to reach the substance of life. Life is but a tissue of habits."

A Case in Point

One particular student of Kabbalah with an agonizing case of obsessive-compulsive disorder successfully rid himself of this affliction. Jeremy (not his real name) explains:

> *As a kid I had an agonizing ritual that I had to perform every night before I went to bed. I would walk into every single room of my*

house and look at the four corners of the ceiling. Then I had to walk into the kitchen and look at all the cupboards to make sure they were closed, and look at all the dials on the oven to make sure they were turned off. Then I had to carefully walk into my bedroom and check my closet, including the four corners of the closet ceiling. After that I looked under my bed. Only then could I climb into bed with peace of mind. If I deviated in any way from this routine, I had to start all over again. Sometimes it took me half an hour before I finally made it into my bed. I remember sobbing as I did this routine every single night, sometimes four or five times until I got it right, because it was so painful. I hated it, but I couldn't stop myself.

Once, when I rode my bike to the candy store, my tire went over a particular crack in the sidewalk. I thought my tire was going to get caught. It didn't, but after that I began to obsess about the crack. I suddenly had a fear about not being able to let go of the thought about the crack. I couldn't get it out of my mind. It stayed with me for years.

I had other obsessive issues. If my hands touched the material on our couch a certain way, I would get the shivers. It would be worse if I bit my nails and then touched the couch. Nevertheless, I felt compelled to bite my nails and rub my hand on the material, torturing myself. It got so bad that I walked around the house with tissue paper wrapped tightly around every finger on both hands so I would not feel any material on the chairs or couches in my home. I slept with socks on my feet for 35 years because I could not stand the feeling of the sheets on my toes. As an adult, I would quickly scan the four cor- ners of a ceiling whenever I walked into a room. I developed a bunch of other small obsessions and behaviors as an adult but *they did not torture me quite so much as the ones I had when I was a kid.*

In my 30s, I began studying Kabbalah. I loved it. It was amazing, and over the years I began incorporating various kabbalistic practices into my life. I began using tools such as the Sabbath connection, which involved certain practices every Friday night and Saturday. I began using prayers every morning and meditating upon The Zohar. And, of course, I kept reading Kabbalah books and studying. One day I realized that my obsessions had vanished without a trace. My compulsive behaviors had disappeared.

I discovered what it meant to be filled with Light because the darkness of OCD that had preoccupied me my entire life no longer existed. I didn't care what my hands touched. I took my socks off when I went to bed (my wife especially appreciated that one) and I fell in love with the feeling of the sheets on my feet. I didn't care any more about the corners in a ceiling. I didn't care what thoughts popped into my mind because I knew they didn't belong to me. When I refused to take ownership of these thoughts (simply by knowing about the existence of the so-called monster) they vanished from my mind. I wasn't worried that something bad was going to happen because I gave up control. A few years later it occurred to me that I simply replaced dark negative habits with positive ones.

Of course I appreciate what Kabbalah did to help me personally, but the greatest reward I received involved my children. When my daughter was seven years old she started washing her hands compulsively. She was developing other rituals that I could see she had inherited from me. So I gave her The Zohar, I explained the concept of the monster

THE **MONSTER** IS REAL

to her, and I taught her how to connect to the 99% Reality. It was over in a few days. Literally. I saw with my own eyes how quickly the Light stamped out the darkness in her life. She never compulsively washed her hands again.

My kids practice habits that generate Light every day. They live peacefully with clear heads and minds free of dark, tormenting habits and anxieties. There are no words to convey my appreciation for what Kabbalah gave us. By the way, my wife never suffered from these types of ailments. Can you imagine how crazy she thought we all were? Can you imagine how happy she is now?

TECHNIQUE #4:
FEAR OF GOD

"The fear of the Lord is the beginning of wisdom."
—Proverbs 9:11

Some televangelists love to preach about "the fear of God." The term implies that because God is so powerful, and sometimes judgmental, you need to be afraid of His wrath.

Kabbalah says this is hogwash!

The force called God is an infinitely positive energy made up of pure happiness and delight. Nothing negative can emerge from such a force. There is nothing to fear from such a force. In fact, this force eradicates all fear from your life.

What then does the Bible mean when it refers to "fear of God," and how can it help you remove your fears of life?

THE **MONSTER** IS REAL

The term *fear of God* is a code. In the original Hebrew version of the Old Testament, the term for *fear of God* is a derivative of the phrase "to see."

What does this mean? What are you supposed to see?

The Laws of Cause and Effect

Kabbalah says that "to see" means to recognize the cause-and-effect principle that governs your life. In other words, for every action, there's a reaction somewhere down the line. It might take minutes, months, or decades to emerge, but for every cause there will be an effect.

So here's the bottom line: Every reactive action has a corresponding negative result. That result is a curtain that conceals the Light and increases your fear. Every proactive act also has an effect, only this time the effect is the removal of the curtain, along with increased Light and serenity in your life.

The problem is this: The monster doesn't allow you to

see the cause-and-effect relationship in life. All the monster shows you is this moment. When you only see the present moment, you react. This creates future chaos in your life.

If you stopped for a second and considered (or "saw") the consequences of your unkind actions before you took them, you'd be motivated to shut down your reaction and become proactive. If you could foresee the repercussions of your selfish and intolerant behavior in the present moment, you'd be inspired to share and be kind to both friends and enemies alike.

Fear of God means seeing the cost and consequences of your deeds before you commit them.

How do you do that?

The Power of Light

If you're locked in a dark room and you want to see, what do you need? A light, naturally. Meditating on the Names of God and *The Zohar* brings you Light. Using the tools of Kabbalah every day elevates your con-sciousness, raises your awareness, and allows you to see and feel more.

All of this helps you to foresee the cause-and-effect relationship that governs this challenging and awe-inspiring game called life. Armed with the knowledge and tools this book has just offered you, courtesy of the ancient sages, you no longer have to play the game filled with fear.

And it won't be!

TECHNIQUE #5:
THE ARI'S TECHNIQUE

The fifth and final technique comes from a great Kabbalist who lived during the 16th century. His name was Isaac Luria. His nickname was *the Ari*, which means *the Holy Lion*.

The Ari was one of the greatest Kabbalists of history. Isaac Newton and some of the greatest thinkers of the scientific revolution studied his writings. That's not surprising, because the Ari revealed secrets of science and medicine that are only now being confirmed by modern-day physics and medical science.

According to the Ari, to banish a fear from your being you should light a candle and sit down with a pencil and a small piece of paper. Write down your fear on the paper, and meditate upon it. Summon forth the feelings and symptoms associated with the fear. Then write down all the emotions and feelings that this fear causes you. Acknowledge to yourself that your own reactive nature, from this life or a past life, is responsible for the manifestation of this fear. Now take the paper and burn it. Try it. Many people get great relief from this simple technique.

FEARS WERE MEANT TO BE CURED, NOT COPED WITH

All of your fears were meant to be 100% cured by virtue of your own personal transformation from reactive to proactive. Transformation means sharing with other people. It means learning how to consider and put the welfare of others ahead of your own self-interest, not for moralistic reasons, but for your deeper well-being. When you do, you will wind up with even more happiness than you ever imagined.

When you change yourself through your own effort, you become responsible for your own joy instead of having the Creator give it to you like a handout. This is how you fulfill your purpose in this world, which is to become the creator of your Light.

To make this transformation challenging, and thus worthy of the Light, the monster (ego) was created to tempt you and seduce you into self-interest and reactive responses 24 hours a day. Each time you react, you create a curtain that dims the Light that awaits you in the 99% Reality.

To fix that reaction infraction, you receive opportunities so you can effect the necessary change of character. Many of those opportunities can be found in your fears.

When you defeat fear, you correct the reaction infraction and tear away the veil that separates you from the 99% Reality. Light is now free to flow to you. And that Light, the force called God, wants to fulfill you even more than you want to be fulfilled.

We just have to stop being afraid of being happy.

If you were inspired by this book in any way and would like to know how you can continue to enrich your life through the power of Kabbalah, here is what you can do next: Read the book *The Power of Kabbalah* or listen to the *Power of Kabbalah* audio tapes.

The Power of Kabbalah

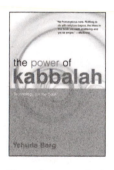

Imagine your life filled with unending joy, purpose, and contentment. Imagine your days infused with pure insight and energy. This is *The Power of Kabbalah*. It is the path from the momentary pleasure that most of us settle for, to the lasting fulfillment that is yours to claim. Your deepest desires are waiting to be realized. But they are not limited to the temporary rush from closing a business deal, the short-term high from drugs, or a passionate sexual relationship that lasts only a few short months.

Wouldn't you like to experience a lasting sense of wholeness and peace that is unshakable, no matter what may be happening around you? Complete fulfillment is the promise of Kabbalah. Within these pages, you will learn how to look at and navigate through life in a whole new way. You will understand your purpose and how to receive the abundant gifts waiting for you. By making a critical transformation from a reactive to a proactive being, you will increase your creative energy, get control of your life, and enjoy new spiritual levels of existence. Kabbalah's ancient teaching is rooted in the perfect union of the physical and spiritual laws already at work in your life. Get ready to experience this exciting realm of awareness, meaning, and joy.

The wonder and wisdom of Kabbalah has influenced the world's leading spiritual, philosophical, religious, and scientific minds. Until today, however, it was hidden away in ancient texts, available only to scholars who knew where to look. Now after many centuries, *The Power of Kabbalah* resides right here in this one remarkable book. Here, at long last is the complete and simple path—actions you can take right now to create the life you desire and deserve.

The Power of Kabbalah Audio Tapes

The Power of Kabbalah is nothing less than a user's guide to the universe. Move beyond where you are right now to where you truly want to be—emotionally, spiritually, creatively. This exciting tape series brings you the ancient, authentic teaching of Kabbalah in a powerful, practical audio format.

You can order these products from our Web site or by calling Student Support.

Student Support: Trained instructors are available 18 hours a day. These dedicated people are willing to answer any and all questions about Kabbalah and help guide you along in your effort to learn more. Just call **1-800-kabbalah**.

MORE PRODUCTS THAT CAN HELP YOU BRING THE WISDOM OF KABBALAH INTO YOUR LIFE

The Red String Book: The Power of Protection
By Yehuda Berg

Read the book that everyone is *wearing!*

Discover the ancient technology that empowers and fuels the hugely popular Red String, the most widely recognized tool of kabbalistic wisdom. Yehuda Berg, author of the international best-seller *The 72 Names of God: Technology for the Soul*, continues to reveal the secrets of the world's oldest and most powerful wisdom with his new book, *The Red String Book: The Power of Protection*. Discover the antidote to the negative effects of the dreaded "Evil Eye" in this second book of the *Technology for the Soul series.*

Find out the real power behind the Red String and why millions of people won't leave home without it.

It's all here. Everything you wanted to know about the Red String but were afraid to ask!

God Does Not Create Miracles. You Do!
By Yehuda Berg

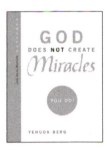

Stop "waiting for a miracle". . . and start making miracles happen!

If you think miracles are one-in-a-million "acts of God," this book will open your eyes and revolutionize your life, starting today! In *God Does Not Create Miracles*, Yehuda Berg gives you the tools to break free of whatever is standing between you and the complete happiness and fulfillment that is your real destiny.

You'll learn why entering the realm of miracles isn't a matter of waiting for a supernatural force to intervene on your behalf. It's about taking action *now*—using the powerful, practical tools of Kabbalah that Yehuda Berg has brought to the world in his international best sellers *The Power of Kabbalah* and *The 72 Names of God*. Now Yehuda reveals the most astonishing secret of all: the actual formula for creating a connection with the true source of miracles that lies only within yourself.

Discover the Technology for the Soul that really makes miracles happen—and unleash that power to create exactly the life you want and deserve!

The Dreams Book: Finding Your Way in the Dark
By Yehuda Berg

In *The Dreams Book*, the debut installment of the Technology for the Soul Series, national best-selling author Yehuda Berg lifts the curtain of reality to reveal secrets of dream interpretation that have remained hidden for centuries.

Readers will discover a millennia-old system for understanding dreams and will learn powerful techniques to help them find soul mates, discover career opportunities, be alerted to potential illness in the body, improve relationships with others, develop an overall deeper awareness, and much more.

The dream state is a mysterious and fascinating realm in which the rules of reality do not apply. This book is the key to navigating the dreamscape, where the answers to all of life's questions await.

God Wears Lipstick
By Karen Berg

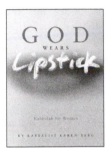

For 4,000 Years, Kabbalah was forbidden to women—until one woman decided that was long enough.

In directing Kabbalah Centres worldwide with her husband, Rav Berg, Karen Berg opened the world's most ancient form of wisdom to everyone on earth—for the first time.

Now, in *God Wears Lipstick*, she reveals women's special spiritual role in the universe.

Based on the secrets of Kabbalah, *God Wears Lipstick* explains the spiritual advantage of women, the power of soulmates, and the true purpose of life, and conducts a no-holds-barred discussion of everything from managing relationships to reincarnation to the sacred power and meaning of sex.

The 72 Names of God: Technology for the Soul™
By Yehuda Berg

The story of Moses and the Red Sea is well known to almost everyone; it's even been an Academy Award–winning film. What is not known, according to the internationally prominent author Yehuda Berg, is that a state-of-the-art technology is encoded and concealed within that biblical story. This technology is called the 72 Names of God, and it is the key—your key—to ridding yourself of depression, stress, creative stagnation, anger, illness, and other physical and emotional problems. In fact, the 72 Names of God is the oldest, most powerful tool known to mankind—far more powerful than any 21st century high-tech know-how when it comes to eliminating the garbage in your life so that you can wake up and enjoy life each day. Indeed, the 72 Names of God is the ultimate pill for anything and every-thing that ails you because it strikes at the DNA level of your soul.

The power of the 72 Names of God operates strictly on a soul level, not a physical one. It's about spirituality, not religiosity. Rather than being limited by the differences that divide people, the wisdom of the Names transcends humanity's age-old quarrels and belief systems to deal with the one common bond that unifies all people and nations: the human soul.

Becoming Like God
By Michael Berg

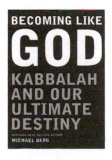

At the age of 16, Kabbalistic scholar Michael Berg began the herculean task of translating *The Zohar*, Kabbalah's chief text, from its original Aramaic into its first complete English translation. *The Zohar*, which consists of 23 volumes, is considered a compendium of virtually all information pertaining to the universe, and its wisdom is only beginning to be verified today.

During the ten years he worked on *The Zohar*, Michael Berg discovered the long-lost secret for which mankind has searched for more than 5,000 years: how to achieve our ultimate destiny. *Becoming Like God* reveals the transformative method by which people can actually break free of what is called "ego nature" to achieve total joy and lasting life.

Michael Berg puts forth the revolutionary idea that for the first time in history, an opportunity is being made available to humankind: an opportunity to Become Like God.

The Secret
By Michael Berg

Like a jewel that has been painstakingly cut and polished, *The Secret* reveals life's essence in its most concise and powerful form. Michael Berg begins by showing you how our everyday understanding of our purpose in the world is literally backwards. Whenever there is pain in our lives—indeed, whenever there is anything less than complete joy and fulfillment—this basic misunderstanding is the reason.

The Essential Zohar
By Rav Berg

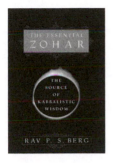

The Zohar has traditionally been known as the world's most esoteric and profound spiritual document, but Kabbalist Rav Berg, this generation's greatest living Kabbalist, has dedicated his life to making this wisdom universally available. The vast wisdom and Light of *The Zohar* came into being as a gift to all humanity, and *The Essential Zohar* at last explains this gift to the world.

Power of You
By Rav Berg

For the past 5,000 years, neither science nor psychology has been able to solve the fundamental problem of chaos in people's lives.

Now, one man is providing the answer. He is Kabbalist Rav Berg.

Beneath the pain and chaos that disrupts our lives, Kabbalist Rav Berg brings to light a hidden realm of order, purpose, and unity. Revealed is a universe in which mind becomes master over matter—a world in which God, human thought, and the entire cosmos are mysteriously interconnected.

Join this generation's premier Kabbalist on a mind-bending journey along the cutting edge of reality. Peer into the vast reservoir of spiritual wisdom that is Kabbalah, where the secrets of creation, life, and death have remained hidden for thousands of years.

Wheels of a Soul
By Rav Berg

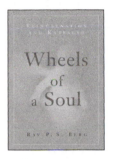

In *Wheels of a Soul*, Kabbalist Rav Berg reveals the keys to answering these and many more questions that lie at the heart of our existence as human beings. Specifically, Rav Berg explains why we must acknowledge and explore the lives we have already lived in order to understand the life we are living today . . .

Make no mistake: *you have been here before.* Reincarnation is a fact—and just as science is now beginning to recognize that time and space may be nothing but illusions, Rav Berg shows why death itself is the greatest illusion of all.

In this book you learn much more than the answers to these questions. You will understand your true purpose in the world and discover tools to identify your life's soul mate. Read *Wheels of a Soul* and let one of the greatest kabbalistic masters of our time change your life forever.

THE KABBALAH CENTRE
The International Leader in the Education of Kabbalah

Since its founding, The Kabbalah Centre has had a single mission: to improve and transform people's lives by bringing the power and wisdom of Kabbalah to all who wish to partake of it.

Through the lifelong efforts of kabbalists Rav and Karen Berg, and the great spiritual lineage of which they are a part, an astonishing 3.5 million people around the world have already been touched by the powerful teachings of Kabbalah. And each year, the numbers are growing!

To the Rav and Karen, and all the Chevre,
with profound gratitude and love,
for revealing the Light
and for being my inspiration.

To my sons, Alain and Kevin Iamburg,
for teaching me the magnitude of unconditional love,
and for the blessing of having you in my life.
May the Light protect you and be with you always.

M.I.